LIVED

ON

SOCIAL

MEDIA

By

Caro Cartier

Copyright Page

Title: Lived On Social Media
Author: Caro Cartier
Publisher: The Moss Magic Publishing LLC
ISBN: 979-8-9867886-5-4

Disclaimer

The views and opinions expressed in this book are solely those of the author, Caro Cartier, and do not necessarily reflect the official policy or position of any other individual, organization, or entity. While every effort has been made to ensure the accuracy and completeness of the information contained herein, the author assumes no responsibility for any errors or omissions, or for the results obtained from the use of this information.

All characters, events, and narratives depicted in this book are fictional. Any resemblance to actual persons, living or dead, or actual events is purely coincidental. The author has used his creative license to craft a narrative that is intended for entertainment and thought-provoking purposes.

The author and publisher disclaim any liability for any loss, damage, or injury incurred as a consequence, directly or indirectly, of the use and application of any of the contents of this book.

Table of Contents

Introduction

Welcome to **"Lived on Social Media,"** a
story that delves into the intertwining lives
of high school students as they navigate the
complex and often perilous world of social
media. This narrative explores the influence
of digital interactions on real-life
relationships and the hidden dangers that can
lurk behind the screens.

In today's connected world, social media
plays a significant role in shaping identities,
forming friendships, and creating
communities. However, with its vast reach
and instantaneous communication, it also
brings forth challenges and threats that can
have profound effects on young minds. This
story is a reflection of those realities, seen
through the eyes of a group of teenagers

whose lives are upended by a mysterious figure known as LIVED.

Brandy, our protagonist, is a typical high school student enjoying her teenage years, filled with friends, school activities, and the occasional drama. Her life takes an unexpected turn when she encounters Damien, a local basketball legend, and becomes entangled in a sinister game orchestrated by LIVED. As the stakes rise, Brandy and her friends must confront their fears, uncover the truth, and fight back against manipulation.

Through the experiences of **Ciera, Lexi, Diana**, and their families, the story highlights the importance of resilience, loyalty, and the strength found in unity. Each character's journey offers a unique perspective on the impact of social media, illustrating both its power to connect and its potential to harm.

"Lived on Social Media" is more than just a tale of teenage drama; it is a cautionary story about the digital age. It reminds us that behind every profile and post is a real person with real emotions, and that the actions we take online can have significant consequences offline.

As you turn the pages, immerse yourself in the world of Brandy and her friends. Feel their struggles, celebrate their triumphs, and understand the profound message about the digital landscape that shapes our lives today.

Welcome to their journey. Welcome to **"Lived on Social Media."**

LIVED

ON

SOCIAL MEDIA

Chapter 1:

The Birthday

Morning

There's a lot of things in life we take for granted thinking "this is what's supposed to happen" or "this is what I want." We forget the amount of effort it takes to make sure the small things are in place to present a large gift or present. Sometimes we get so self-centered that we don't think about others consider the love our surrounding circle of family and peers have for us.

Your date of birth should always be special no matter if you're male or female, young or old, black or white. People are born every day of the year but your day is your day, and it should be a big celebration. Who doesn't want a birthday party with all their friends and family members singing that familiar phrase "Happy Birthday to you, Happy Birthday to you, Happy Birthday to you" with cake, candles, food, and gifts? The birthday song is legendary and has been the same for centuries. Some have added beats to it or more words and rhythms, but the main words and arrangement will never change.

Everybody loves music and a party, but when it's time to sing Happy Birthday, it's all about you. "All eyes on me," in my 2Pac voice. So make sure it's special: special outfit, special shoes, hair beat, face beat, and ready to accept all the love. But what do you do when you're turning 16 and your parents still treat you like you're 10, especially when you're daddy's baby girl?

Like Brandy, who was born 15 years ago, and her birthday is this weekend for her Sweet Sixteen. Brandy is a very popular young lady on social media, in school, and in her city. Everybody knows Brandy.

Brandy's father walks into her room at 6:10 am to turn off her alarm clock that's been going off for 10 minutes. Brandy was so tired that not only did she not hear the alarm clock at 6 am, she also didn't hear her father open her door to her bedroom. Her father shook her shoulder several times, saying, "Wake up, baby girl. You're going to be late for school."

Brandy woke up saying, "OK, daddy, I'm up."

Her father replied by saying, "I'm cooking breakfast for you; do you want pancakes or waffles?" But before Brandy could answer, she realized that she still had on her clothes from last night under the covers. She quickly pulled the covers from her neck to her nose and replied, "Pancakes, daddy, pancakes."

Her father closed the door and walked out, thinking, hmm, that was strange. Why did she snatch the covers over her face like that? What's my baby girl up to? Not knowing Brandy went out last night with her friends, didn't come home until 1 am, and still had on her short skirt, revealing shirt, and wristband from the party. Yeah, daddy's little girl is up to no good.

Chapter 2:

Secrets and Social Media

Parents will always be 10 steps behind when it comes to their children. It's getting harder and harder to keep up with the life of a child. There are things parents will never know or find out about because most parents don't communicate with their kids. Some parents would rather talk at their children instead of talking with them, dictate orders versus discussing situations.

Even though this story might expose a few true secrets, parents should come to the realization that times are changing and raising kids does not come in a book or a step-by-step guide/manual. Each child is different. Study them and raise them day by day, not when you find time. Most parents use the old school saying, "I've already done what you're going to do," but how is that when you were born over 20 years before your child? These are not those days and times.

Brandy should not be sneaking out of the house at the age of 15. If something bad happens, then how would her parents know where to start looking? Brandy thinks she is more mature than 15. She feels like she can handle herself and is ready to see the world, but if she only knew what kind of life-threatening challenges are waiting for her on the road she is traveling on. SMH, it's about to get real!

Chapter 3:

Morning Routine

Brandy gets up and ready for school, but first posts a message on social media so her 5K friends can see: "Pops almost found out #lastnight." In 5 minutes, she received 200 comments, 300 emojis, and 2K likes. This lil girl's page was poppin! One of her friends left a comment saying, "We was lit," and Brandy replied with a heart emoji.

Facebook will only allow you to have 5K friends, but every time Brandy posts something negative, she gets a friend request from someone named LIVED. After someone else posted, "Girl, yo daddy need to let you grow," Brandy replied with, "Right, let me live, pops!"

The second she replied, she got a like, heart emoji, and another request from the page LIVED. Brandy replied @LIVED, "Thanks, but I can't add you. I have too many friends, sorry," with a wink emoji. LIVED replied, "Hit accept," with a sad face emoji. Brandy clicks on the accept button and even though she had 5K friends already, the request was accepted.

Running behind, Brandy threw her phone on the bed and continued to get dressed for school. She ran to the kitchen to eat those fluffy buttermilk pancakes her dad made for her. As soon as she sat at the kitchen table, her dad said, "There's my baby girl, all ready for school and to get all good grades," with a large smile on his face. Brandy smiled back and said, "Yes, daddy, it's all about that 4.0 GPA. The principal said she wants to meet with you and moms to talk about college."

"OK, baby girl. I'll let you know when she gets off work."

"OK, daddy, please do because moms be trippin'. She thinks my principal likes you."

"Oh yeah, baby girl, your principal trying to get in a higher class. LOL."

"Yeah, daddy, she trying to get upgraded. LOL. Naw, baby girl, she ain't ready for this history lesson."

"Right, daddy. Moms gone' give her that math 5+5 with an exponent of 3. LOL."

"Dang, baby girl, that's a lot of hands."

"Yeah, daddy, mommy keeps that Draco."

Chapter 4:

School Drama

Brandy gets dropped off at school where one of her friends, Ciera, was waiting outside talking to a group of kids about the party last night.

"Thanks for the ride, daddy. See you later. Let me catch up with Ciera."

"OK, baby girl. Tell your best friend I said hi and y'all be good today."

"OK, daddy. Love you. Hey, Ciera, my daddy said hi!"

Ciera heard Brandy and ran over to the truck to hug Brandy and speak to her daddy.

"Heyyyy, daddy!"

Brandy gave Ciera a mean mug and pulled her away from the truck fast. Ciera said, "Dang, best friend, I'm speaking to daddy." Brandy pulled Ciera close and told her,

"Bitch, don't get yo teeth knocked out."
Ciera told Brandy, "Bitch, don't get mad at
me 'cause yo daddy a snack. Shit, I'm
hungry." Brandy said, "OK, bitch, keep
playing with yo fronts." They both walked
into the school together laughing, but Ciera
had something on her mind.

Chapter 5:

Classroom
Troubles

While sitting in class, Ciera sent Brandy a text message, but Brandy was working on a problem the teacher wrote on the board asking for the hypotenuse of a ladder if a wall was 12 feet tall and the ground was 10 feet long. Brandy feels her phone vibrating and notices Ciera sent her a text stating, "I fucked up, best friend," so she replied, "Bitch, what you do," and went back to solving the problem.

Every student in the class was waiting on Brandy because she was the smartest in the class next to Ciera. These two young ladies were more than popular, they were the whos who. Ciera was so distracted sending Brandy another text that she couldn't solve the problem. When Brandy looked at the next message from Ciera, her eyes got big, heart started beating fast, and body went numb. Ciera's message said, "When I dropped you off last night, I put that Henny bottle in your trash can by the driveway." Brandy replied, "WTF you do that for, pops takes the trash out every morning." As soon as she pushed send, she received a picture message and a text from her daddy. The pic was of the empty Hennessy bottle and the text said, "We need to talk." Now her dad was searching her room instead of going to work.

Chapter 6:

Parental Confrontation

When Brandy's mother pulls in the driveway, she notices her husband's truck door open and the trash can next to the door. Her mother was curious and questioned what's going on. Did something happen to her husband because the back door was also wide open? She quickly ran in the house and screamed her husband's name, "Anthony! Anthony! Oh God, Anthony, are you here?"

Anthony answered, "Yes, babe, I'm in Brandy's room."

The mother ran into the room and asked her husband, "Bae, is everything okay? What's going on? Why are you searching Brandy's room?"

Anthony looked at his wife, holding a leather mini skirt, a bottle of Hennessy, and a torn bra. Brandy's mother instantly was pissed. She said, "Anthony, please tell me it ain't what it looks like," and her husband said, "Brasia, it's exactly what it looks like, and she can't lie about this."

Brasia texted Brandy, "I know yo lil ass ain't drinking and wearing stripper clothes," then joined her husband in searching her room. Brandy received her mother's text and started shaking because she knew, even though she was daddy's baby girl, momma will beat her ass and deal with dad later. Brandy was nervous, so nervous she couldn't concentrate on solving the next problem of $f(x) = 2x^2 + 3x - 6$ with a value of $f(2)$, so Ciera solved it with the answer 8.

Chapter 7:

Social Media Confession

Brandy laid her head on her desk and did what most teenage Americans do when they're upset, happy, or bored: express their feelings and emotions on social media. But as history has presented time and time again, everything is not for social media. Never put your personal business online, yet people still do it every day. Brandy posted, "Parents found Henny bottle from last night thanks to dumb dumb BF and now on my line like the Feds SMFH." Again, she got 3k likes, 500 comments, and an inbox from LIVED asking, "Are you good HML."

Brandy was scared because her mother sent a picture message of the mini skirt, wristband, and condoms with a message saying, "Bring yo ass straight home…" LIVED sent her a sad face emoji to her inbox, saying, "HML if you need an ear I'm here." Brandy replied, "I hate my life right now SMH." LIVED responded with, "Aww don't feel like that. I'm a part of your life now. Things will get better. Don't hate me, we just met."

Brandy replied, "No, I don't hate you, just tired of being treated like a baby. I'm almost grown."

LIVED replied, "What you mean almost grown? You look mature to me in your profile pic. Don't tell me this is catfish."

Brandy replied, "LMFAO thanks for the laugh. No, no catfish. This really me. I'll be a whole 16 this weekend, GROWN WOMAN!" while texting and walking down the school hallway.

Chapter 8:

Friends and
Enemies

Before Brandy could read LIVED's next message, she was greeted by Diana and Lexi. Diana said, "Bitch, say word, we just read your post."

Lexi said, "Damn, you about to be under full investigation."

Diana pulled Brandy into the girl's bathroom, followed by Lexi. Diana told Brandy, "Okay, first off, where yo bestie at, 'cause she out of control for yo, you need a real bestie," cut off by Lexi.

Brandy told both Lexi and Diana, "Y'all calm down 'cause what we ain't gone do is talk about my friend from 5th grade!!"

Diana looked at Brandy, then looked at Lexi and started laughing with Lexi as they walked towards the sink and mirror. Then

Lexi asked Brandy, "Not she protecting her LOL."

Brandy said, "Yo damn right," walking to the third mirror. "That's my BFF."

Diana said, "So tell us what happened 'cause that party was too lit."

Brandy said, "Girl," and before she could tell the story, Ciera walked out of the bathroom stall, saying, "I left the Henny bottle in her trashcan when I dropped her off then."

Brandy asked Ciera, "Why? Why would you do that to me, Best Friend?"

Ciera started crying and gave Brandy a hug, saying, "I didn't want to get pulled over with an empty bottle, bestie. I'm so sorry." So they both cried while hugging each other.

Chapter 9:

Drama Unfolds

Lexi and Diana looked at each other and fell out laughing. Lexi told Diana, "Man, these hoes need a show."

Diana said, "Right, Dumb bitches gone wild."

Lexi said, "Naw, uh uh, Love N Sad Hoes."

Diana said, "Wait, Lexi, my phone ringing. Hello, yeah, this Diana. Who is this? Jerry. Jerry who? Springer. Yeah, Jerry, we got two to go, right."

"My bestie set me up, show filming live on fox!!"

Brandy told them, "Y'all hoes tired."

Ciera said, "Don't worry, bestie, they gone get whooped."

Diana and Lexi walked out of the bathroom laughing more, singing the verse from Yo Gotti & Lil Baby, "Put a date on it."

"Bitches always talking that tough shit, Bitch, put a date on it."

"Bye, hoes."

Brandy told Ciera, "Don't worry about them," and put her phone on the sink to look in her purse. When Brandy's alert went off, Ciera picked up the phone and saw an inbox from LIVED.

"Bitch, you talking to randoms now."

Brandy said, "Girl, he cool. I just added him."

Ciera said, "Yeah, I see you got 5001 friends. How you do that? Let me see what he want. Oh, he said, 'Cheer up. We all go through hell of a days, but I'll handle the flaws with you. Ttyl.'"

"Damn, that was a hot verse. He must rap."

Brandy snatched her phone and said, "Girl, you need to work on what you gone tell my parents."

Chapter 10:

Ciera's Dilemma

Ciera said, "Hold up, what you mean what I'ma tell yo parents? I can't meet yo momma. She might find out about us."

Brandy said, "Yes, you are 'cause they already know, so you have to say that bottle was left in your car by yo older brother 'cause he be driving yo car and I was supposed to throw the condoms away. I got it from there."

Ciera told Brandy, "Girl, that just might work, but what she gone say when she see that look in yo daddy's eyes when he see me."

Brandy said, "Bitch, will you be serious. My birthday is Saturday, and I can't have no drama right now."

"OK, Brandy, OK. I got you, bestie. What you want me to do?"

Brandy told Ciera, "Just answer the phone when I call and remember that the Hennessy bottle and condoms were in your car and I was supposed to throw the condoms away like you threw the bottle away. I got you, bestie. You know Ce Ce and Be Be 4 Life, plus I'ma be your stepmomma soon."

Brandy said, "I'ma let you have that 'cause I need yo ass, but you owe me big time for getting me in trouble."

They walked to the gym where there was a basketball game going on, so they sat on the bleachers to watch and look cute until the last hour bell rang to leave school.

Chapter 11:

The Basketball Court

Damien was coming down the court just passing the half-court line, dribbling the ball. He was coming up against another student trying to take the ball from him, so he dribbled the ball through his legs then behind his back. This made the other student trip over his own feet and fall. As soon as the student fell, everybody in the gym went crazy with screams and laughter, so Brandy looked up at Damien as he was going towards the rim. Brandy liked what she was seeing.

Damien was popular as well. He was a basketball legend on the courts of high school. Six feet, one inch tall, slim but muscular, so he was cut up. He was so in shape that Brandy asked Ciera, "Girl, who is that action figure?"

Ciera told Brandy, "Girl, that's Damien. Every girl in this school wants him."

Brandy asked, "What's his name on IG and Facebook? I'ma do some lurking."

Ciera told her, "Girl, you trying to use them condoms for that saucy sixteen, ain't you?"

Brandy said, "Mind yo business, plus those got confiscated, remember." "I want him though."

LIVED sent Brandy another inbox while she was looking for Damien's page asking, "WYD," but Brandy didn't see because she was too busy searching for Damien's page.

Chapter 12:

Research and
Rebound

While Brandy was searching for Damien's page, Ciera was searching for LIVED's page to do her homework on him. Meanwhile, Brandy's parents were searching her room. One of the players grabbed the rebound and passed the ball to Damien but overthrew the ball, so that made Damien race to the ball that just so happened to land in Brandy's lap.

Damien reached for the ball asking Brandy, "Let me get that."

Brandy told Damien, "How bad do you want it?" while spinning the basketball on her finger.

Damien was caught off guard but always on top of his game, so he responded with, "I don't want what's not mine."

Brandy said, "So you don't want it?" while tossing the ball from one hand to the other. This made Damien say, "I'm not into games, so you can keep it," then ran over to the ball cage and grabbed another basketball. Brandy was embarrassed and still holding the basketball, looking at Damien play the rest of the game. This made her want him even more. She was used to male students chasing behind her, looking to get her attention, so the way Damien was acting was the opposite of her normal male interactions. Ciera hit Brandy on her leg and said, "Damn bestie, you looking thirsty."

Chapter 13:

Thirst for Attention

"Naw, never that," said Brandy. "I'm on his line though. Think he can just ignore me? Who he think he is."

Ciera said, "We can pull up on his ass bestie."

"Naw, best friend, calm down. I just found his page. He only got 200 friends, so he can't be too important."

The 3:30 pm bell rings to let the kids out of their last hour class and Damien went to the cage to return the second basketball so he can change and leave, but Brandy walked up behind him with the first basketball and told Damien, "Here go your ball back."

Damien looked at her and said, "Thanks," and grabbed the ball.

Brandy told him, "You know I was just playing with you," but Damien quickly responded with, "You're too cute to play games. That's what kids do." She just stood there staring at him as he walked away. She was even more determined to get his attention, so she went back to his page and sent an inbox. Brandy noticed an unread message from LIVED asking, "WYD," so she replied with, "Leaving school. Had a bad day and should get course when I get home." There she goes again putting her personal business on social media.

Chapter 14:

Social Media

Sympathy

LIVED sent a post and tagged Brandy in it, saying, "My heart goes out to my friend Brandy. She's having a bad day #healasoul," and out of his 5K friends, he received 5K likes with comments like all black hearts, fire emojis, #soulsearching, and "We got u Brandy" messages. When Brandy clicked on the post and saw all the love she had on LIVED's page, she was flattered and put "Thanks everybody" on the post. Then she inboxed LIVED, "Thank you, you're a sweetheart." He replied with, "I got you."

Ciera made a left turn off the main street with Brandy in the passenger seat and pulled into Brandy's driveway at the same time her father was coming out of the back door. Brandy's dad was disappointed in his baby girl. His image of her was damaged, so he kept walking towards the back patio to clear his mind. Brandy got out of the car and took six steps but stopped and told Ciera to come with her.

Ciera said, "Girl, I'm not going in your house." Brandy grabbed the door handle, but Ciera hit the lock button and said, "No, bitch, I'm going home."

Brandy didn't know her mother was standing in the front doorway, but Ciera knew. Brandy hit Ciera's door window telling her, "So you really not coming, Ce Ce," but Ciera was looking at the anger in Brandy's mother's eyes.

Chapter 15:

Parental Confrontation

Brandy's mother screamed her name, "Brandy, bring yo lil fast ass in this house now!!"

Brandy turned around and saw her mother's face and quickly hit Ciera's glass three times, "Bam, bam, bam." "Girl, get out and come with me," but Ciera started the car and put it in reverse and said, "Bitch, um hell to the no." Brandy stomped her foot and said, "Cece, come on," and pulled the door handle. Ciera said, "Bitch, move. She walking towards us."

Brandy's mom said, "Brandy, if I have to call yo ass again, I'ma come snatch the soul out yo ass. Get in this house NOW!!"

Brandy started walking towards her mother, sniffling and crying with her head back and arms folded, but as soon as her mother reached for her, she took off running to the backyard, screaming, "Daddy, daddy!!" Her daddy was sitting in his lawn chair, and Brandy ran up and put both arms around him, crying and heart beating fast, saying, "Daddy, I'm sorry. Please help me, daddy, please!"

Brandy's mother walked up on the patio deck and said, "Anthony, let her go. She got some explaining to do."

Anthony said, "I can't move, Brasia. This my baby girl," and Brandy said, "Save me, daddy," but moms told the dad, "Now don't make me beat both of y'all then call 911 'cause I done killed you."

Chapter 16:

Family Matters

Anthony told the mother, "What I tell you about playing like that?" but the mother cut him off quick, saying, "I'm from East St. Louis, bra, the land of potholes, ditches, and scotches. Ain't no playing around here. Move and let her go."

The father said, "Ain't doing that, and you most forgot I'm from Charlie park, so act goofy if you want to. Brandy, tell us what happened. Brasia, shut up and sit yo tuff ass down."

Brandy told her story of how they snuck out at night and went to a party and noticed Ciera's brother left a liquor bottle in the car with a box of condoms, so they threw the bottle away to keep from drinking with it, and she kept the condoms to ask her mother about safe sex. Daddy looked at his daughter with tears in his eyes, asking, "What about the mini skirt? Because that's not a good look, baby girl."

She said, "Daddy, I'm sorry. I wanted to outdo the other girls. They be calling me a square."

Daddy grabbed his daughter and hugged her tight, saying, "Aww, my poor baby girl."

The mother folded her arms and just shook her head, then said, "Anthony, she got you wrapped around her finger. If you believe that story."

Anthony said, "Why would she lie, Brasia?"

The mother said, "Cause she ducking this ass whoopin."

Chapter 17:

Truth and Consequences

"Let's call Ciera and find out. Brandy, let me see your phone and see if she tells the same story."

Brandy said, "No, daddy, don't put my bestie in this. Her brother gonna be pissed about her telling his business."

The mother said, "Now, Anthony, you don't think they already put this story together? I was a young 15-year-old before. I used to be fine and trying to be grown."

The daddy said, "What you mean used to be fine? Girl, you still a dime. I married a supermodel with yo too sexy for them clothes ass. Stand right there. Let me take yo pic and post it on my Facebook page and show the world my gorgeous queen."

The mother said, "OK, take it I'm ready, daddy said damn that ass PHAT. Now let's take some more in the bedroom."

Brandy said, "Y'all nasty. Hope y'all use them condoms y'all found."

The mother said, "Girl, you lucky I love yo daddy. He just saved that ass. Come on, Anthony, and set your R&B playlist on your phone."

Brandy sat on the patio deck and pulled out her phone to post what just happened on Facebook. "Just got a pass #NO TIME #Free Da Guys."

Ciera posted on Brandy's page, "Call me bestie ASAP."

Brandy wrote back, "You cut off @Ciera." LIVED and 800 people hit like and the only comments were from Diana, saying, "Aww shit, let me grab my popcorn. The movie bout to start."

Lexi commented, "I see, I see. I heard their theme song playing, Sad and Bougie, two bitches looking real stoopid. LMAO."

Brandy didn't respond, nor did Ciera, but LIVED inboxed Brandy asking, "Who are Diana and Lexi?"

Brandy responded, "Some nobodies. Them hoes sad and messy. I hate them."

LIVED replied, saying, "Hate is a strong word."

Brandy responded with, "They always messing with me. I'm tired of them."

People say some harsh and hurtful things these days not knowing the consequences of our actions. The social media platform allows people to vent like they are writing in a diary, but the events in your personal thoughts you typing on your personal phone to your personal page does not mean it's private. The entire world can see what your venting about, and yes, they will judge you, attack you, and use your personal thoughts as a joking matter.

LIVED took it upon himself to inbox Diana and Lexi about bothering Brandy, saying, "Ima need y'all to fall back with Brandy."

Lexi quickly responded with, "Who are you?"

Lexi called Diana right after, asking her, "Girl, who is LIVED?"

Diana said, "I don't know. Why?"

Chapter 18:

Confrontation Online

Lexi said, "Cause he just inboxed me talking about fall back off Brandy dumb ass."

Diana said, "Bitch, are you for real?"

Lexi told her, "Yeah, I'm bout to check that ass."

Diana said, "I got an inbox from him too, but I blocked him and deleted the message. Just block his ass."

Lexi is a hot head, so she said, "I ain't ducking no wreck. I'ma check that ass!" Lexi told LIVED, "Who the fuck are you all in my inbox talking about fall back?"

LIVED responded, "I am who I am. Like yo man said in the bible, my name speaks for itself."

Lexi responded aggressively by saying, "Well, I don't give a fuck who you are. Fuck you and Fuck Brandy."

LIVED said, "Find out who you're talking to before speaking reckless and crash."

Lexi said, "Boy, FUCK YOU. I smoke over here. Don't catch it and choke."

LIVED replied, "Y'all love quoting rap verses and slick lines. Lol. I'll give you a lifetime of smoke."

Lexi replied, saying, "Location."

LIVED said, "I'll meet you in Hell with yo tuff ass."

Lexi said, "I stay in the first room on the first floor, bitch. Hell is my second home."

LIVED didn't respond, so Lexi screenshot the conversation and sent it to Diana. Diana responded by saying, "LMFAO SMH. Girl, block him now!!"

Chapter 19:

Research and
Regret

While Ciera was at home waiting for Brandy to call, she continued Google searching for LIVED but couldn't find anything but a few video posts from people describing their personal experiences with similar outcomes. One video was last year, and the young lady was recording herself while putting on makeup, talking about how she met a guy named LIVED and he gave her all sorts of expensive gifts. Another video was from the same young lady's mother speaking at a news conference outside of a mental institution about her daughter's latest physical and mental condition. She was just sitting in a chair, alive but lifeless, with no emotions.

Ciera was doing her homework on the people trying to be a part of her best friend's life. She also dissected Damien's page, looking for a girl in his life but couldn't find any, and that's when Brandy called.

Ciera answered, "Hey, bestie."

Brandy said, "Miss me with all that. You left me stranded when I needed you."

Ciera said, "I'm sorry, bestie. I was scared of your moms. She was looking like she on one."

Brandy replied with, "She was, but my daddy saved me. Now, what you want?"

Ciera said, "Dang, bruh. I said I was sorry, and I can't find this dude named LIVED on social media."

Chapter 20:

The Mystery Deepens

Brandy said, "Why you looking for him? What you on?"

Ciera said, "Damn, a little overprotective, ain't you? What y'all got going on?"

Brandy said, "He cool, but Ciera wanted to know who he was and how did Brandy get 5001 friends, and nobody else can go over 5K. Ciera changed the subject from LIVED to Damien and asked Brandy what y'all was talking about at that ball cage."

Brandy said, "I sent him an inbox. Let me see if he responded. He on my hit list."

Damien replied to Brandy's inbox, saying, "Hi, Brandy, what's up."

Brandy got excited and hung up on Ciera so she could focus on Damien, saying, "Bitch, I'll call you back."

Brandy sent Damien a response, "I just wanted to talk to you. Do you want to talk?"

Damien responded, "Yeah, we can talk. What's on your mind?"

Brandy said, "You."

Damien sent a reply, "Why am I on your mind? Brandy, don't you have more important things to do."

Brandy said, "I just want to apologize for playing with you in the gym."

Damien said, "It's cool. I accepted your first apology. We good. I be focused on the court making sure I go pro."

Brandy replied, "My bestie already told me all eyes on you in town, but why you only got 200 friends."

Damien asked, "Why do you have 5K? Do you know all those people because I know every one of my 200."

Brandy thought about what Damien just asked her because she didn't know all those people. She only knew 50 personally. She replied with, "Why you say 5K? I have 5001."

Damien said, "I see 5K. That's the limit, and you never answered my question. Do you know all of them, or do you need internet fame."

Brandy said, "I only know 50, and no, I don't need internet fame."

Damien asked, "So why entertain people you don't know." Brandy was stuck again. She couldn't answer Damien's question. She wasn't used to straightforward questions from people her age, so she just didn't respond. Instead, she called Ciera back and told her, "Girl, guess who I just talked to."

Ciera said, "Who and why you hang up on me."

Brandy said, "Damien sent me a message, and I didn't want to keep my new bae waiting."

While Brandy was on the phone with Ciera, her father walked up behind her and waved at Ciera while on FaceTime. Ciera's face expression changed and said, "Oh shit, heyyy, daddy." Brandy turned around and saw her mother & father.

Her father said, "Ciera, I have some questions for you," and Ciera quickly said, "OK, daddy, anything for you. What you want to know?"

That's when Brandy's mother snatched the phone from Brandy and told Ciera, "Look here, lil girl. First off, stop flirting with my husband before I reach through this phone."

Ciera said, "Yes, ma'am." Brandy's mother was not playing. She told Ciera, "Go put a shirt on. My man don't want to see your bra."

Ciera said, "Yes, ma'am." After she put her shirt on, she came back to the phone. Then Brandy's mother asked her, "Now, where that Henny bottle came from, and yo ass bet not lie."

Ciera said, "That was my brother's. He left it in my car, so I put it in your trash can, and I'm sorry."

Brandy's mother said, "I don't want to hear that sorry shit. Did Brandy get those condoms from you?"

Ciera said, "Yes, ma'am," and started crying. "I told her to do it to throw them away, and she wanted to ask y'all about safe

Brandy said, "Y'all nasty. Hope y'all use them condoms y'all found."

The mother said, "Girl, you lucky I love yo daddy. He just saved that ass. Come on, Anthony, and set your R&B playlist on your phone."

Brandy sat on the patio deck and pulled out her phone to post what just happened on Facebook. "Just got a pass #NO TIME #Free Da Guys."

Ciera posted on Brandy's page, "Call me bestie ASAP."

Brandy wrote back, "You cut off @Ciera." LIVED and 800 people hit like and the only comments were from Diana, saying, "Aww shit, let me grab my popcorn. The movie bout to start."

Lexi commented, "I see, I see. I heard their theme song playing, Sad and Bougie, two bitches looking real stoopid. LMAO."

Brandy didn't respond, nor did Ciera, but LIVED inboxed Brandy asking, "Who are Diana and Lexi?"

Brandy responded, "Some nobodies. Them hoes sad and messy. I hate them."

LIVED replied, saying, "Hate is a strong word."

81

Brandy responded with, "They always messing with me. I'm tired of them."

People say some harsh and hurtful things these days not knowing the consequences of our actions. The social media platform allows people to vent like they are writing in a diary, but the events in your personal thoughts you typing on your personal phone to your personal page does not mean it's private. The entire world can see what your venting about, and yes, they will judge you, attack you, and use your personal thoughts as a joking matter.

LIVED took it upon himself to inbox Diana and Lexi about bothering Brandy, saying, "Ima need y'all to fall back with Brandy."

Lexi quickly responded with, "Who are you?"

Lexi called Diana right after, asking her, "Girl, who is LIVED?"

Diana said, "I don't know. Why?"

Chapter 21:

Confrontation Online

Lexi said, "Cause he just inboxed me talking about fall back off Brandy dumb ass."

Diana said, "Bitch, are you for real?"

Lexi told her, "Yeah, I'm bout to check that ass."

Diana said, "I got an inbox from him too, but I blocked him and deleted the message. Just block his ass."

Lexi is a hot head, so she said, "I ain't ducking no wreck. I'ma check that ass!" Lexi told LIVED, "Who the fuck are you all in my inbox talking about fall back?"

LIVED replied, "I am who I am. Like yo man said in the bible, my name speaks for itself."

Lexi responded aggressively by saying, "Well, I don't give a fuck who you are. Fuck you and Fuck Brandy."

LIVED said, "Find out who you're talking to before speaking reckless and crash."

Lexi said, "Boy, FUCK YOU. I smoke over here. Don't catch it and choke."

LIVED replied, "Y'all love quoting rap verses and slick lines. Lol. I'll give you a lifetime of smoke."

Lexi replied, saying, "Location."

LIVED said, "I'll meet you in Hell with yo tuff ass."

Lexi said, "I stay in the first room on the first floor, bitch. Hell is my second home."

LIVED didn't respond, so Lexi screenshot the conversation and sent it to Diana. Diana responded by saying, "LMFAO SMH. Girl, block him now!!"

Chapter 22:

Research and Regret

While Ciera was at home waiting for Brandy to call, she continued Google searching for LIVED but couldn't find anything but a few video posts from people describing their personal experiences with similar outcomes. One video was last year, and the young lady was recording herself while putting on makeup, talking about how she met a guy named LIVED and he gave her all sorts of expensive gifts. Another video was from the same young lady's mother speaking at a news conference outside of a mental institution about her daughter's latest physical and mental condition. She was just sitting in a chair, alive but lifeless, with no emotions.

Ciera was doing her homework on the people trying to be a part of her best friend's life. She also dissected Damien's page, looking for a girl in his life but couldn't find any, and that's when Brandy called.

Ciera answered, "Hey, bestie."

Brandy said, "Miss me with all that. You left me stranded when I needed you."

Ciera said, "I'm sorry, bestie. I was scared of your moms. She was looking like she on one."

Brandy replied with, "She was, but my daddy saved me. Now, what you want?"

Ciera said, "Dang, bruh. I said I was sorry, and I can't find this dude named LIVED on social media."

Chapter 23:

The Mystery Deepens

Brandy said, "Why you looking for him? What you on?"

Ciera said, "Damn, a little overprotective, ain't you? What y'all got going on?"

Brandy said, "He cool, but Ciera wanted to know who he was and how did Brandy get 5001 friends, and nobody else can go over 5K. Ciera changed the subject from LIVED to Damien and asked Brandy what y'all was talking about at that ball cage."

Brandy said, "I sent him an inbox. Let me see if he responded. He on my hit list."

Damien replied to Brandy's inbox, saying, "Hi, Brandy, what's up."

Brandy got excited and hung up on Ciera so she could focus on Damien, saying, "Bitch, I'll call you back."

Brandy sent Damien a response, "I just wanted to talk to you. Do you want to talk?"

Damien responded, "Yeah, we can talk. What's on your mind?"

Brandy said, "You."

Damien sent a reply, "Why am I on your mind? Brandy, don't you have more important things to do."

Brandy said, "I just want to apologize for playing with you in the gym."

Damien said, "It's cool. I accepted your first apology. We good. I be focused on the court making sure I go pro."

Brandy replied, "My bestie already told me all eyes on you in town, but why you only got 200 friends."

Damien asked, "Why do you have 5K? Do you know all those people because I know every one of my 200."

Brandy thought about what Damien just asked her because she didn't know all those people. She only knew 50 personally. She replied with, "Why you say 5K? I have 5001."

Damien said, "I see 5K. That's the limit, and you never answered my question. Do you know all of them, or do you need internet fame."

Brandy said, "I only know 50, and no, I don't need internet fame."

Damien asked, "So why entertain people you don't know." Brandy was stuck again. She couldn't answer Damien's question. She wasn't used to straightforward questions from people her age, so she just didn't respond. Instead, she called Ciera back and told her, "Girl, guess who I just talked to."

Ciera said, "Who and why you hang up on me."

Brandy said, "Damien sent me a message, and I didn't want to keep my new bae waiting."

While Brandy was on the phone with Ciera, her father walked up behind her and waved at Ciera while on FaceTime. Ciera's face expression changed and said, "Oh shit, heyyy, daddy." Brandy turned around and saw her mother & father.

Her father said, "Ciera, I have some questions for you," and Ciera quickly said, "OK, daddy, anything for you. What you want to know?"

That's when Brandy's mother snatched the phone from Brandy and told Ciera, "Look here, lil girl. First off, stop flirting with my husband before I reach through this phone."

Ciera said, "Yes, ma'am." Brandy's mother was not playing. She told Ciera, "Go put a shirt on. My man don't want to see your bra."

Ciera said, "Yes, ma'am." After she put her shirt on, she came back to the phone. Then Brandy's mother asked her, "Now, where that Henny bottle came from, and yo ass bet not lie."

Ciera said, "That was my brother's. He left it in my car, so I put it in your trash can, and I'm sorry."

Brandy's mother said, "I don't want to hear that sorry shit. Did Brandy get those condoms from you?"

Ciera said, "Yes, ma'am," and started crying. "I told her to do it to throw them away, and she wanted to ask y'all about safe sex. I'm so sorry. Please forgive me. That's my bestie."

Brandy's mother told her, "Ciera, stop all that crying. Ain't nothing wrong with you," and gave the phone back to Brandy. Ciera saw Brandy and said, "Girl, yo momma mean as shit. Tell her I'm sorry."

Brandy's mother heard Ciera and said, "Don't be sorry. Be careful." Ciera hung up the phone. Brandy told her mother, "Woman, you scared my bestie. She just hung up." Her mother said, "So fuckin' what," and walked out of the room. Brandy whispered to her father, "Thank you, daddy, for saving me." Her father said, "Just promise me you won't rush into growing up. Stay my baby girl for a while."

Chapter 24:

Parental Guidance

Every parent is entitled to raise their children the way they see fit. They belong to you, but always remember we are their teachers. They learn from us, so the way you raise them as children most of the time will be the result of adulthood. I know this question will touch a few households, but it needs to be said. Does a child under the age of 12 need a cell phone? I say no because between 1 and 10, you, as an adult, still have a lot of influence on your child's life, and giving them a cell phone to occupy their time and attention allows them to receive growing lessons from the internet. Google, YouTube, then click on whatever video pops up first—that's what your child is learning. If you don't have time for your child, then make time! I know the world is hard, and life has no mercy, but you found time to make that baby, so find time to raise it. Teach it responsibility, manners, correct pronunciation of words, reading, math, and all the necessary elements and skills to survive. Monitor your child's social media page. There are too many predators online. Just because they send you a friend request does not mean they are friendly.

Chapter 25:

The New Enemy

LIVED sent Diana and Lexi a friend request, but Diana blocked him, so hers didn't go through. Lexi looked at hers and hit accept so she can do her homework on his page. She sent him an inbox saying, "Now you want to be my friend." LIVED didn't respond, so this made Lexi send another inbox saying, "Say something with yo friendly ass. Don't get quiet now."

LIVED responded, "Thanks for accepting my request. You still want smoke?" Lexi is so much of a hot head that she let her temper control her actions and emotions. She hates being ignored and loves to fight. You have to wonder why does this girl have so much anger each time to herself.

LIVED struck a nerve, so she replied, "Bitch, I thought you had a lifetime of smoke. Run that location."

LIVED started smiling to himself, saying, "I like this lil girl," smh, and sent a reply, "We will meet soon. Just fall back on Brandy, like I said."

Lexi said, "What, you her people or something? Did she send you at me? I'ma crush that hoe."

LIVED didn't reply just yet. He found Lexi funny and showed the people around him. They all smiled and sent her friend requests. Lexi saw she had over 1500 friend requests all of a sudden and said, "Damn, my shit popping today. Let me take a selfie and post it."

Chapter 26:

Social Media Escalation

Lexi accepted all 1500 requests, then posted a selfie of her holding up two middle fingers with the caption, "Fuck This World. I'll be here when the smoke clears," and all 1500 of her new friends hit like. Plus, LIVED left a comment of smoke emojis and flames.

Lexi replied to LIVED's comment with three skull emojis, three gun emojis, and three fire emojis.

Diana saw Lexi's post and called her. When Lexi answered, Diana said, "Bitch, delete that pic. That ain't how we move."

Lexi said, "Bitch, I just got 1500 likes in 30 seconds."

Diana said, "No, you don't. I only see 2 likes."

Lexi said, "Bitch, you jealous 'cause my page popping."

Diana said, "Lexi, delete that post," but Lexi was so in her feelings about LIVED that she told Diana, "Bitch, I'm tired of this clown ass motherfucker."

Diana said, "I told you to block him. Don't make me come get yo phone. Lexi, delete that post and block him." While Lexi was deleting her latest post, she still had fire in her eyes, plus thinking Diana was jealous of all her likes. Blind anger is worse than built-up anger, and Lexi had both.

Diana saw that Lexi deleted the pic and sent her a text saying, "I'm worried about you. I'm bout to pull up so we can talk."

Ciera told her, "Bitch, pull up then. I'm at home. Bring some chips and juice."

Chapter 27:

Chips and Juice

The city of St. Louis has Red Hot Ripplets and Old Vienna Sundance Chips that are addictive, and every store in East St. Louis sells them. They go good with an orange or grape Vess soda, but if you really want to get a house hood taste, try the Red Hot Ripplets with a 50-cent honey bun, just glaze and no white icing. Open the bag, crunch up the chips, and dip the honey bun in the crumbs and take a bite.

Lexi was waiting on Diana, but she could not confront LIVED's page for some reason, so she just left it alone and turned the radio on station Hot 104.1 FM. The DJ shouted out Brandy's name to promote her birthday party her father put together for her, "Don't miss the most anticipated party of the year with a live performance by [redacted] for my girl Brandy's Sassy Sixteen B-Day Bash."

Brandy heard the commercial and ran into her parents' room while they were naked and laying in bed. Brandy was screaming, "Daddy, daddy, you got [redacted] coming to perform for my birthday!!" She was so excited that she didn't even notice they were in the middle of having sex.

Her mother said, "I almost cancelled that party. You better not act up for the next 5 years. Do you hear me?"

"Yes, ma'am. Yes, ma'am. I promise, mommy. It's bout to be lit for my B-Day. Oh wait, why y'all naked? Where are y'all clothes at? Ew, eww, what was y'all doing in here. Y'all nasty. I'm gone!"

Chapter 28:

Birthday Preparations

Ciera called asking, "Is it real, best friend? Is it real? I heard the commercial on the radio."

Brandy said, "Yep, bitch. We outside this weekend. We need outfits. Pick me up. Let's go to the mall."

As soon as Brandy walked out of her parents' room, her father's phone started ringing. It was Brandy's principal. Her daddy answered while putting his robe on and threw the phone speaker in a quiet room.

A female voice said, "Hello, is this Brandy's father?"

He said, "Yes, who am I speaking with?"

"This is the high school principal from your daughter's school. Are you busy?"

He said, "A little bit. How can I help you?"

She said, "I'm calling about your daughter's future." The mother was acting like she wasn't listening but was tuned in. Anthony said, "I'm listening. Is she doing good in school?"

The principal said, "Actually, yes, she's doing wonderful. She needs to start looking at colleges because it's looking like she will get bumped up a grade."

The father said, "Oh yeah, that's good news, principal."

The principal cut him off and said, "Please call me Janae. Everyone does."

Brandy's mother said, "Bae, who is that woman you're talking to?"

He said, "Janae, the principal at East Side."

The mother said, "Principal what? She calling your phone for?"

The father said, "Hold on, Janae," and put the phone on mute, then asked his wife, "Are you OK?"

The wife said, "Um no, I want to know why she calling yo phone when my number is the only number on file and what's this Janae shit. Y'all on a first name basis?"

"Bae, you doing too much. Calm down and let me talk to this lady about our daughter."

The wife said, "You got 5 minutes."

Anthony pushed the mute button, but what he didn't notice is that he never pushed mute the first time, and the principal heard everything, so he hit mute twice and said, "Are you still there?"

The principal said, "Yes, I am. I thought you hung up on me." Anthony didn't know what to say because his wife was looking at him and carefully listening.

The principal said, "I want to mail a few college applications and flyers to your address, or should I drop them off personally?"

Anthony said, "You can mail them," but the principal felt like being petty and said, "Are you not interested, Anthony? I can be there in 5 minutes."

Anthony said, "Just mail it, and I'll talk it over with my wife when we receive it."

Chapter 29:

Tension and Distraction

"OK, I'll dress it up and make sure it's attractive and irresistible and tell wifey I said hi."

Anthony said, "OK, thanks again," but Janae said, "Where you going? Why you rushing me off the phone? I want to talk some more."

Anthony started sweating and moving around, looking nervous. He asked the principal, "About what?"

Janae said, "Do I get to pick the topic or whatever comes to your mind about your daughter's principal."

Anthony said, "No, I'm good," and wiped his face, feeling his hand on his forehead, and said, "Thanks, Ms. Principal."

She said, "I thought I told you to call me Janae."

Anthony said, "You did."

Janae said, "Well, say it before you hang up, or should I come over and ask you in person."

Anthony got up from sitting on the bed and walked to the bathroom and grabbed his toothbrush, but Janae was not letting up. She said in a soft voice, "Anthony, say my name for me. Say it, say it." Anthony then she did a quiet moan. Anthony dropped the toothbrush in the sink while holding the phone to his ear with his shoulder. His hands were shaking, and saying, "I can't, I don't, I can't." Janae had enough fun and said, "Bye, Anthony. Hang up and kiss wifey for me."

Anthony hung up and turned around to find his wife staring at him, saying, "What that bitch say 'cause you ran in here looking spooked, bra."

"Nothing, bae," said Anthony. "She's mailing college apps and flyers to the house for Brandy. Now go lay yo ass down and take those back off or get them ripped off."

Brasia said, "Damn daddy, OK, come rip them off then, hubby. Lock the door this time and turn that phone off."

Chapter 30:

Secrets and Shadows

Later on that night, Brasia woke up and jumped in the shower, but when she pulled the covers back, she woke up her husband, Anthony. Anthony looked at the alarm clock on the nightstand and noticed it was going on 10 PM. They had slept the rest of the day away, but he smiled at his wife while she walked from the bed to the bathroom naked. Now don't get it twisted, just because Brasia had a temper and didn't play no games when it came to standing up for herself doesn't mean she was busted or should I say bad-looking. Don't let the outside viewers' low expectations of East St. Louis people blur your thoughts and vision of how the women look. Yes, East St. Louis is the hood. Yes, East St. Louis is rated the underdog. Yes, East St. Louis has its corruption.

But if something jumped off, people will form together like the old TV show Voltron and get on your ass. Brasia was the old school but still household phrase: Dime Piece P.H.A.T. (Pretty, Hot, And Tempting) or Bad Bitch. She turns heads when she walks, so leaving the bed going to the bathroom instantly turned Anthony on. Plus, Brasia made sure her business was taken care of. She was always on top of her game. Anthony got out of bed and followed her to the shower; this is one woman he couldn't resist. Have you ever had that one? You don't have to say it out loud. I don't want you to read this book and get in trouble, smacked in the head, or punched on. We will keep that secret in the book. But I know you got one; I won't tell. Everyone has a person that they just can't resist whenever they see them or hear their name; nothing else matters. Your heart stops, you just stare and visualize y'all being together. Go ahead, I'll give you 30 seconds to reminisce, think of that person, and come back to this paragraph. Go ahead, I'll wait… OK, welcome back! Let's get back to the story.

Chapter 31:

Morning

Preparations

After Anthony left the shower to get dressed, his wife stayed in to take another from the shower sex. Brandy just walked in the house from the mall with Ciera walking behind her.

Ciera said, "Girl, you sure it's safe to come in?"

Brandy told her, "Yeah, you good," and they both headed towards Brandy's bedroom, bumping into Anthony, Brandy's father, in the hallway.

Anthony told Brandy, "I see you went shopping again," and Brandy said, "Yep, daddy, it's B-day behavior. I have to be right."

Anthony hugged her. His daughter realized he was worried about something. Brandy could feel the concern from her father, so she said, "Daddy, don't worry. I'm still your baby girl."

Ciera was just looking and quickly said, "Aww, ain't that cute and precious," so Anthony spoke to Ciera, and of course, she replied with, "Hey, daddy, I want a hug too," but Brandy snatched her arm and pulled her to the room and closed the door. Anthony just shook his head and walked away towards the kitchen. He pulled out a skillet, added some butter, and opened a loaf of bread with four slices of cheese. While he was making him and his wife grilled cheese sandwiches, she was coming out of the shower admiring herself in the mirror and noticed her husband's cell phone was on the nightstand. Now we all know that's a no-no because you know what's about to happen.

Chapter 32:

Suspicion and Jealousy

Especially if you're up to no good. If you're doing anything on your cell phone you don't want your mate to find out about, then either keep it with you or put a code on it. Now in this case, nothing was going on. Anthony was faithful to his wife. He was one of those dudes who always wanted to be married and take care of his family. There's an old saying that most women use that states, "All men cheat," but that's not true and only comes from those who have been cheated on because they always think men cheat, so they think cheating on them is the answer, but that's not how relationships go.

Brasia didn't think her husband was cheating, but she did remember that conversation between Anthony and the principal and how he was looking—dropped the toothbrush, stuttering, sweating, wiping his face, and pacing the floor. Yep, the whole time he was on the phone, she was looking and listening. She reached for the phone to see what number she called from because when she enrolled her daughter in school, she gave her cell number for the contact. So why was the principal calling her husband's phone, and how did she get his number?

When she picked up the phone, she saw the last number, and it was not the number from the school. So Brasia said, "I know this bitch ain't calling from her personal cell phone."

Chapter 33:

A Shared History

Brasia was a bad bitch, but so was Janae, the principal. They knew each other before Brandy was born, before Anthony, before their high school years. Yes, Brasia and Janae had history and had beef with each other since junior high school. They both ran track and both were cheerleaders back in the day, always going against each other. So calling her husband's phone was going to be a repeating issue. Brasia went to the number and sent a text message saying, "Thanks for calling. Can't wait to talk again," but Janae peeped the game and responded, "You're more than welcome. Your daughter is a great student, but let's only talk during professional business hours."

Brasia read the message and smiled, then deleted the text and put the phone down.

Meanwhile, Brandy and Ciera were in the room discussing what Ciera found online about LIVED. He was the topic of the night because Diana and Lexi were doing the same at Lexi's house. But what they didn't know is LIVED was watching all four of their pages and decided to inbox Brandy, "Hi friend, I need to show you something." Brandy's phone lit up, alerting her of a message.

Chapter 34:

Unexpected Revelation

When Brandy read the message, she showed it to Ciera, and Ciera told her, "How come every time we talk about him, he inbox you?"

Brandy said, "I don't know."

Ciera said, "Ask him what he got to show you. It better not be no freaky stuff."

Brandy responded, "Hi, LIVED. Wyd and what you want to show me?"

LIVED responded to Brandy, "I'ma show you that I got yo back like I told you at first." Then he sent a screenshot of him and Lexi arguing online. When Brandy saw the message, she said, "What the fuck," and let Ciera see.

Ciera grabbed her phone and posted on her page, "If anybody got problems with my bestie, they can get it @Lexi." This was a direct message to Lexi, and after the post got 300 likes, Lexi responded with, "Bitch, calm yo goofy down b4 yo show end." Now 300 likes turned into 1500 and 800 reposts and tags.

Ciera sent another response, "This bitch run around all day barking like a poodle. Pit Bulls over here, hoe." Lexi responded with, "I tame wild dogs, bitch. Respect this goon. You don't want it." Ciera said, "Bitch, I'm begging for it. What's a goon to a goblin."

The post was up to 4K likes and 5K reposts and tags. Everybody was watching, and LIVED sat back laughing.

Chapter 35:

The Showdown

Lexi responded, "Wya hoe. Location. You don't want this smoke."

Ciera posted, "I'm where you want me to be, BITCH. Name it."

Lexi posted, "Smoke on the school parking lot, goof."

Ciera posted, "OMW. What you sent, LIVED?"

Lexi posted, "Bitch, fuck you. Fuck LIVED, and fuck Brandy. OMW."

Ciera ran out of Brandy's house and jumped in her car without telling Brandy. Lexi put Diana out of her parent's house and jumped in her car. Both were headed to the school parking lot. LIVED was watching and said, "Oh shit," laughing even more and grabbed all his people and headed to the school parking lot. Somebody called Brandy and said, "Go to Ciera's page now. It's going down." Then somebody called Diana and said, "Go to Lexi's page. It's going down." Everybody in the city was pulling up to the school parking lot. The night security guard called the principal, and she jumped up and called the police. She received a text about Lexi and Ciera fighting online and meeting at the school, so she jumped in her truck and headed to the school. LIVED had all his people headed that way, saying, "Damn, I love this shit."

Chapter 36:

Intervention

Diana called Brandy because what y'all don't know is that they are cousins, but their mothers, who are sisters, don't get along. Diana said, "What's up, cuz? I think Ciera and Lexi about to fight at school."

Diana said, "Yeah, I know. We need to stop them."

Diana said, "I'm picking you up so we can go together."

Brandy said, "OK, come on. I'm ready."

LIVED made it there first to get front-row seats with all of his people. The school parking lot was packed and ready to live stream the fight. Ciera pulled up and walked to the middle of the crowd screaming, "Where this hoe at?"

The principal pulled up while trying to call Ciera's parents and Lexi's parents but no answer, so she called Brandy's father's phone. Brandy's father's phone rang, but he was watching TV. His wife saw the number and grabbed the phone, saying, "Janae, why the fuck you calling my husband's phone?"

Janae answered, "Brasia, girl, where's yo daughter 'cause Ciera and another student about to have a big fight at the school."

Brasia ran in her daughter's room and saw she was gone, then looked out the window and saw Brandy get in Diana's car. Brasia told Janae, "She gone. I'm on my way down there, but bitch, we need to talk." Then she hung up and ran out the door.

Chapter 37:

Parking Lot Chaos

The crowd was deep with all their headlights on. The security guard was waiting on backup, and LIVED and all his people were instigating in everybody's ear. Lexi pulled up and saw the crowd and got charged even more. She jumped out and headed to the center, looking for Ciera. LIVED yelled out, "Woop that bitch," and the crowd repeated, singing the song from the famous movie Hustle and Flow, "Woop that bitch, woop that bitch, woop that bitch."

Brandy and Diana pulled up and both ran to the middle of the crowd to find Lexi and Ciera going in a circle like two boxers in a boxing ring. Ciera said, "Yep, got that ass now."

Lexi said, "Swing, hoe."

Ciera hit Lexi with a right hand and grabbed her hair with the left. Lexi caught the first blow and moved in close to hit Ciera in the mouth with a right, but Ciera hit Lexi with two rights while holding Lexi's hair. Lexi shook it off and hit Ciera with one right and a quick left. They both took a step back to gather their fight stance when Brandy grabbed Ciera and Diana grabbed Lexi to break it up. The police lights and sirens were pulling up, so everybody got in their cars and pulled off.

Chapter 38:

Police Arrival

The police tried to block off both exits, but people were driving through the grass, getting away. The principal pulled up and saw the chaos, parked, and got out to talk to the police. Brandy's mother pulled up looking for her child and saw the principal talking to the police but no Brandy. Brandy was standing by the tree going off on Ciera while Diana was going off on Lexi. LIVED was still there loving every minute of it; he was ducked off laughing. The security guard came out of hiding and ran over to the principal and officer, breathing hard, saying, "Man, I'm glad y'all showed up and handled this side because I had the other side covered."

Brasia walked up to the principal and tapped her on the shoulder, saying, "Hey, where's my daughter?"

Janae, the principal, said, "I don't know. I just pulled up."

The officers pointed at the three cars left on the lot and started walking towards them. It was Brandy, Diana, Ciera, and Lexi, so Brasia said, "That's my daughter and niece," and ran over there in front of the officer.

The principal said, "Thanks for your assistance, but we got it from here." The officer waited around and sent the other squad cars back to the station.

Chapter 39:

Emotional Confrontations

The principal said, "You girls have some explaining to do," and as soon as LIVED saw Brasia and Janae, his eyes got big. LIVED knew the two ladies very well, so well that he remembered how he knew them and where from.

Brasia asked Brandy, "Are you OK?"

Diana said, "Hi, Tee Tee Brasia," and Brasia responded, "Hi, baby. Are y'all OK?"

They both said, "Yes, ma'am," and she directed her attention to Ciera and gave her a mean look. Ciera took a step back and put her head down; she knew she was in trouble.

The principal noticed a tall, muscular man standing in the shadows and said, "Hey, you over there, come here. Come out so I can see your face," but LIVED took off running and said, "Let's go." That's when the entire shadow that covered the south side of the lot went behind him. It was that many with him, over a hundred.

The principal said, "Hey, Brasia, grab Brandy and Ciera and leave. I'll take Diana and Lexi with me because I don't know who all those people were standing in the dark."

Brasia said, "Let's go now!!"

Brandy rode with her mother, with Ciera and Diana following her, and so was the principal and Lexi. But the night guard and the officer saw how LIVED and his followers were running in the darkness and went to confront them.

Chapter 40:

Officer and Night Guard

"Hey, hey, all of you, stop running. Stop now," but they couldn't catch them. LIVED told two of his followers to go take care of them, so they stopped and turned around and started walking towards the night guard and the officer.

The night guard said, "Two of them turned around. What should we do?"

The officer pulled his gun out, but the night guard only had a flashlight.

The night guard said, "Give me a gun."

The officer said, "Where yours at?"

The night guard said, "How they coming towards us? Give me a gun!"

The officer said, "Halt, or I'll shoot."

The night guard said, "Halt? Man, what you mean, halt? Shoot they ass, bra."

The officer said, "You can't just shoot people, idiot. I said stop. Stop where you are!" But the two men kept walking towards them, so the officer shot in the air. This made one figure go to the left and the other go to the right.

The night guard said, "Aw man, they just split up. Stop shooting in the air, dumb ass. Go shoot them."

The officer said, "Man, stop acting like a bitch, and you take that one on the left, and I'll take the one on the right."

The night guard said, "With what? A flashlight? Man, I'm out of here," and took off running.

The officer said, "A man, where you going? Come assist me."

The night guard said, "Man, fuck you," and kept running.

Chapter 41:

Homecoming

Brasia made it home and walked into the house with Brandy, Ciera, and Diana. Anthony was still sitting in front of the TV watching an old TV show called "Sanford and Son." Brasia told the girls to go in the den and wait for her while she made a call. All three girls sat down, and Ciera started crying. Brasia went to get her husband's phone to call Janae and told her to meet her at the house with Lexi.

Anthony noticed she had his phone and asked, "Brasi, why do you have my phone?"

Brasia gave Anthony a look and said, "Because I got it. Is there a problem?"

Anthony said, "Nope," and went back to watching TV.

Chapter 42:

The Truth Comes Out

Brasia walked back into the den and told the girls, "I need y'all to tell me what happened and tell me the truth."

Brandy said, "Ciera, tell her."

Ciera said, "Who, me? Girl, uh uh," and shook her head.

Diana spoke up and said, "Tee Tee, my friend was talking crazy about Brandy on social media, and I checked her saying we don't move like that, so I take it that Ciera seen it."

Brandy said, "No, some guy named LIVED sent me a screenshot of him arguing with Lexi about me."

Brasia said, "So all of this is over Facebook beef? Wow. Okay, keep going."

Chapter 43:

The Messages

Brandy said, "I showed the messages to Ciera."

Diana said, "I told Lexi to leave it alone and to block LIVED, but she's so hot-headed I can't tell her nothing sometimes."

Brandy said, "I feel you, cuz, because Ciera's a hot head too."

Brasia stopped them both and said, "Let me see the messages."

Brandy gave her the phone, and Brasia said, "Wow, oh wow, damn, wow, she's going toe to toe with this guy. Now where's the beef with her and Ciera, Brandy?"

Brandy said, "Go here, ma, and click on Ciera's page."

Ciera said, "Girl, why you showing her my page?"

Brasia said, "Hush, lil girl. I'm gonna get on you next. Let me read this text. Oh wow, wow, oh shit, what the, damn, shit, Ciera, you ain't backing down, are you?"

Ciera put her head down and got quiet.

"Lil girl, don't you hear me talking to you?" Brasia said.

Ciera raised her head with tears in her eyes and said, "But Brandy my bestie and Lexi was talking trash like she always does, and I'm tired of her mouth. And don't nobody disrespect my bestie. I love your daughter like she my sister, and I'm so sorry. I'm sorry. Please don't keep me away from her, please."

Chapter 44:

A New Sister

Brasia walked over to Ciera and gave her a big hug. Brasia told her, "First off, look at me and wipe your eyes, girl. I want to thank you for taking up for my daughter and going hard; you are a true friend. I had my doubts about you, but now I see the love you have for Brandy. Stop shaking, Ciera; it's okay."

Brandy said, "Ma, she's scared of you."

Brasia said, "Ciera, from now on, you're my daughter, and I will accept you as Brandy's sister, so relax."

Ciera said, "For real? Are you serious?"

Brasia told her, "Just promise me one thing, Ciera: stop flirting with my man. Cause the way you acted tonight, I'm 10+ times that."

Ciera's eyes got big, then the doorbell rang. Brandy went to the door and let her principal and Lexi in.

Chapter 45:

Lexi's Turn

Janae said, "Hi Brandy, where's your mother?"

Brandy said, "Follow me in the den."

Lexi pulled Janae's arm and said, "Is this safe?"

Janae said, "Yes, we need to get to the bottom of this tonight."

As they both walked into the den, Lexi and Ciera locked eyes, and Ciera stood up. Lexi said, "Round 2, ho."

Ciera said, "Be careful what you ask for."

Brasia told Ciera to sit down, and Janae told Lexi to sit down.

Chapter 46:

The Principal's Inquiry

Brasia told Janae what she read on Brandy's phone and the story the girls told her. Janae was shocked that two of her 4.0 students would act like this. Janae said, "Lexi, this is your time to tell your side of the story."

Lexi said, "I don't want to disrespect your house and nobody, ma'am."

Brasia said, "You say what you need to say."

Lexi said, "Brandy sent some dude to harass me, and I ain't no weak bitch."

Janae said, "You will not use that kind of language, and Brandy, is this true?"

Brandy said, "No, I don't have any male friends."

Janae said, "Who is the dude, Lexi?"

Lexi said, "Some dude named LIVED. Here, I'll show you the first message."

Janae grabbed Lexi's phone and showed it to Brasia. Brasia said, "That's the guy the girls said sent Brandy a text of him and Lexi arguing."

Janae said, "Sounds like y'all got played by this guy named LIVED. He targets all of y'all, but Lexi, you're the one who went for the bait."

Lexi said, "So Brandy, you don't know him?" and Brandy said, "No."

Lexi said, "I hate being played; all my life people have been playing me: my father, my mother, my family, my pastor, my friends."

Diana said, "I ain't never played you. I'm trying to help you because I know how your life is."

Chapter 47:

Emotional Breakthrough

Lexi fell to her knees and started crying. Ciera ran over, got on her knees beside her, gave her a hug, and cried with her. Diana joined in, then Brandy, Janae, and Brasia all gave Lexi one big group hug. Lexi started screaming, "I hate my life, nobody loves me." Even though all of them were hugging Lexi, they could all feel her shaking with rage.

The principal, Janae, told Lexi, "I'm escorting you home because there's more to this story, and I want to know. Let me call the officer from the fight tonight."

Janae called the officer, but he didn't answer, so she called the station to get a police escort to Lexi's house. Brasia grabbed Lexi's arm, wiped the tears from her face, then Ciera told Lexi, "I'll be your friend."

Lexi looked at Ciera and said, "You not mad at me?"

Ciera said, "No, sisters fight all the time, but from now on it's us four against the world."

Lexi smiled and gave Ciera a big hug. Brasia said, "You staying here tonight; we can deal with your issue tomorrow. Is that cool with you, Janae?"

Janae said, "Yeah, I agree, but walk me to the door. I need to run something by you."

Chapter 48:

Reflections and Revelations

Brasia walked Janae to the door and opened it, then asked her, "What's up?"

Janae said, "Girl, I just got a flashback of how me and you used to fight during school."

Brasia said, "Yeah, I remember that was us all day."

Janae said, "But remember how it started? Think back."

Brasia said, "Bitch, are you serious right now? I do remember, and I knew that LIVED name sounded familiar."

Janae said, "Yep, that's the same name that had us trying to kill each other."

Brasia said, "Wow, this shit is fucking crazy."

Janae walked out the door and said, "Bitch, I'm about to find out who this man is because me and you were best friends before LIVED showed up, and now he's playing the same games with kids 15 years later. I hate we aren't friends no more."

Janae opened her truck door, put one leg in, and looked at Brasia in her doorway but didn't see the grown woman married with a child Brasia. She saw teenage Brasia, the Brasia she was best friends with during junior high school 15 to 20 years ago. Brasia watched Janae get in her truck and was reminiscing as well, then Janae pulled off, and Brasia closed her door.

Chapter 49:

LIVED's Lair

While the girls sat in the den at Brandy's house and bonded, LIVED and his followers were at his location laughing and drinking. LIVED said, "Everybody raise your cups and toast to a good night." LIVED was excited, he was so excited that he started dancing and reciting words to a rap song.

LIVED pulled one of his followers to the side. All the other followers were enjoying the music and drinks. LIVED asked him, "Did you record the fight?" and the follower said, "From beginning to end, boss."

The follower he was talking to was named Owen, but his nickname was "O." O was a big muscular guy who had a major temper and was the second son of LIVED. LIVED was no doubt a troublemaker, and his kids were the spitting image of him. His first son wanted to be more active but did not play games with anyone. His temper was shorter than LIVED's, but he knew how to control it. LIVED told O to post the video and tag Ciera and Lexi with #WorldStar and make sure the caption says "LIVED in an East St. Louis fight."

"Where's your brother at, O?"

O said, "I don't know. You know he be doing his own thing."

LIVED said, "I'll find him, don't worry. I need to see where his head is at."

Chapter 50:

The Principal's Search

The principal walked into her house, logged on to her computer, and started searching for LIVED. She ran into the same problem Ciera ran into when she did her searching: nothing but the video of the parent speaking outside of the mental hospital about her daughter. Janae called the hospital and asked about the girl, but the only info they gave her was that she was there, and no other information could be given. So she contacted the mother and asked her about her daughter's condition.

The mother, whose name was Sharon, was talking in a soft voice and told the principal, "My baby hasn't been the same ever since she met a guy named LIVED. He got in her head so much that me and her father couldn't tell her nothing. She came home one day with a diamond necklace, then a diamond ring, then I started noticing her wardrobe changing. I told her I want to meet this guy named LIVED, and she told me he was a good friend and gives her whatever she wants. I thought she was doing drug deals at first, but she swore that would never happen. My baby was a straight-A, 4.0 student with athletic skills like the Olympics, but LIVED destroyed all of that."

Janae asked if she could come talk to her and her husband in the morning.

Chapter 51:

A Mother's Grief

Mother Sharon told Janae, "That would be fine with me, but her father is no longer with us."

Janae said, "I'm sorry to hear that. I know that was devastating for you and your daughter."

Sharon said, "Yes, it was, mostly for our daughter."

Janae asked, "Were they extremely close?"

Sharon said, "Yes, but she was the one who killed him. She's been in the hospital ever since."

Janae was speechless. After Sharon hung up the phone, she got up from the couch and slowly walked into the kitchen to check on the food she was cooking. She reached into the cupboard, pulled out three plates, opened the silverware drawer, and pulled out three forks and three knives. Then she walked to the dinner table and prepared three spots. Sharon walked to her daughter's bedroom and knocked on the door, saying, "Baby, wake up. Your food's ready." Then she knocked on her bedroom door, saying, "Sweetheart, come eat. I'm setting the table."

Sharon was in a daze, and ever since her daughter killed her husband, she refused to accept the fact that they are no longer there. She sat at the table after filling each plate with fried chicken, white rice and butter, and green beans. She took a bite of her chicken and drank some Kool-Aid like her family was still there. But that call from Janae made her face reality, and she cried and hit the floor like the scene from the show "Good Times" when James died.

Chapter 52:

Breakfast at Brandy's

Meanwhile, at Brandy's house, she and the girls were bonding to the point where everything was coming out. All four girls were like sisters now, and with Ciera and Lexi swinging for the same team, there was no beating them.

The next morning, the girls were so exhausted that they were all asleep in the den when Brandy's father woke up and passed by heading towards the kitchen. It was 7 AM and also Brandy's birthday. Brandy's dad saw she had company, so he made sure he made enough pancakes, scrambled eggs, turkey sausages, and grits for everyone. Brasia walked into the kitchen around 7:30 AM, and the sound of the skillet sizzling with that familiar breakfast smell made her stomach growl. She greeted her husband with "Good morning, bae," and kissed him on his jaw.

Anthony said, "Oh no, uh uh, bare toothpaste."

Brasia said, "Boy, stop that," and started laughing.

Brasia hit Anthony on the head and said, "I already handled that," while rubbing his lower stomach. Anthony finished cooking and made Brasia a plate and prepared four more. He told Brasia, "I didn't know we had company."

Brasia bit a piece of sausage, reached for a scoop of grits, and said, "Yeah, bae, it was crazy last night. I had to go down to the school for a fight and make sure our baby was good."

Anthony asked, "Was Brandy fighting?"

Brasia said, "No, but it was about her. It ended with us having three more daughters."

Chapter 53:

A Pony for
Brandy

Anthony asked, "Should I be worried?"

Brasia said, "No, I got it under control, bae."

Anthony told Brasia, "Okay, good. Well, I'm done in here, so I'll be back. I'm going to pick up my baby girl's gift for her party tonight. I know she will love this gift."

Brasia said, "I thought you just booked the venue for the concert for her. What gift did you buy?"

Anthony replied, "A pony so her and her friends can ride."

Brasia looked at Anthony and said, "Anthony, I know you didn't buy no damn pony for your daughter's 16th birthday," but Anthony was dead serious, and yep, he was grabbing his keys and headed out the door.

Brasia called his name, "Anthony, I know you hear me. Anthony!"

Anthony said, "What's up, bae?"

Brasia told him, "You better not bring no fuckin' pony to this party and embarrass this girl."

Anthony walked out anyway. Brasia went into the den to wake the girls up so they could eat and get themselves together. They all rose their heads while stretching and yawning, but Brandy couldn't wait to grab her phone to see all the birthday wishes from her 500 friends.

Brandy told her mom, "Good morning, ma," and went right back to her phone.

Ciera got up, hugged Brasia, and said, "Morning, Ma." Lexi did the same.

Diana said, "Morning, Tee Tee. My momma said call her."

Chapter 54:

Birthday Messages

Brasia told Diana, "Okay, I'll call her now. Y'all go in the kitchen and eat."

Brandy was all smiles while looking at her page and smiled even harder when she saw the inbox from Damien saying, "I see today is your birthday, so I wanted to send you a special wish from me to you. So tell me, what's your wish?"

Brandy ran into the kitchen and started dancing with her phone in hand, saying, "I just got a birthday wish from Damien."

Ciera said, "For real, bestie!"

Diana asked, "Brandy, who? Damien from school?"

Lexi said, "Girl, get that tag, that tweet, that post."

Ciera said, "Yep, sis, in that order."

The mother, Brasia, said, "Who is this Damien?"

All four girls were so excited, so Brasia said, "I take it that he is fine."

Brandy said, "Ma, fine ain't the word."

Ciera said, "Ma, every girl in the school wants him."

Lexi said, "In the city."

Diana said, "In the state."

Brasia said, "Damn, baby girl. Okay, okay."

Brandy showed everybody the inbox and asked, "What should I say?"

Lexi said, "I know you not serious right now."

Diana said, "Right."

Brandy said, "What y'all mean?"

So Ciera snatched Brandy's phone and replied to Damien's inbox with the word "Yooo" and pushed send.

Chapter 55:

Getting Real

Brandy asked, "Ciera, why you do that? I'm not thirsty. He's gonna think I'm easy."

Ciera said, "Bestie, you can't play that hard-to-get role with a dude like that."

Lexi said, "Right, girl, go get what you want."

Diana said, "Right, bag that, tag that, post that."

Brasia said, "Y'all sound like sisters already."

While the girls were eating, they all got a post from LIVED. Brandy's inbox said, "I heard about the fight, new friend. Are you okay?"

Ciera's inbox said, "I see you got hands, but I think she said you soft."

Lexi's inbox said, "You couldn't handle that smoke last night, but you got heart. I like you. HML."

Diana's inbox said, "You have a blocked message from LIVED."

Brasia told Brandy to let her see her

Chapter 56:

A History of Conflict

Brasia said, "This is true, but back then we had AOL (America Online), and it was a dial-up service and always lost connection on MySpace."

Brandy asked, "Ma, what's AOL, MySpace, and dial-up?"

Brasia said, "Before your time, sweetheart. Just stay away from him, let us deal with LIVED."

Janae said, "It was like he knew we were talking about him, because every time we mentioned his name, he would call."

Just then, Janae's phone rang. "Ring, ring, ring," everybody got quiet as Janae answered, "Hello?"

It was the night security guard. "Hello, boss lady, what's up?"

Janae said, "Man, why you calling private, Calvin?"

Calvin said, "Um, because I don't want you to have my number."

Janae said, "But I'm your boss."

Calvin said, "And what that mean? I don't know you like that."

Janae said, "Calvin, I just texted your number, so I already have it."

Calvin said, "No you don't, that's my momma's cell phone."

Janae said, "Wow, I need to know what happened after I left last night. I'm looking for the chief. He's not answering."

Calvin said, "It's Saturday, boss lady. Don't nobody want to talk to you."

Janae said, "Calvin, I'm serious. Stop playing so much."

Calvin said, "Shit, I don't know. I took off running, and he ran the other way towards the scary people like in the movies."

Janae said, "And you left him?"

Calvin said, "Yep, I sure did. It was 20 or 30 of them. Then two started running towards us, so I thought about it: face the thugs for this check or go to the Bottoms Up strip club and spend a check. Hmm, get beat up or go beat something up. Ha ha ha."

Janae said, "Calvin, I don't want to hear that nasty stuff."

Calvin said, "The stripper did. Ha ha ha, she say she like my night stick."

Janae said, "Where is the chief? No one has heard from him."

Calvin said, "Look, boss lady, I don't know. Last time I seen him, he was shooting in the air at the thugs. I only had a flashlight with low batteries."

Janae said, "Calvin, you're fired. Don't worry about coming Monday."

Calvin said, "Wow, on my day off? You really gone fire me on my day off like the movie Friday?"

Janae said, "Yep. Bye, Craig," and hung up.

Chapter 57:

LIVED's
Retaliation

While Janae was calling the chief and Brasia was calling her husband Anthony, LIVED sent Lexi a reply saying, "You ain't on my level, lil girl. Go play with your dolls before I send them demons at you."

He also replied to Ciera, "Don't get touched, half-pint. You ain't big enough to swing with me."

They both were pissed. Both had short tempers. Both looked at each other and knew each one received a message. Lexi sat by Ciera and whispered, "We sisters now, right?"

Ciera said, "Yeah, bitch, what's up? He sent you another message too?"

Lexi said, "Yep, and I got a plan. I want to give it to this slick-talking old man."

Ciera said, "What's the plan?"

Lexi said, "Let's get him to pull up somewhere and beat the shit out of his old ass."

Ciera said, "I'm with it, sis. It's us against everybody."

Lexi replied to LIVED, "I already heard about your old ass. You can't fuck with me, grandpa. You or your dusty demons. Told you 'bout this smoke."

Chapter 58:

The Encounter

LIVED didn't like being called old, so Lexi hit a nerve. LIVED replied, "Lil bitch, you playing with fire."

Lexi replied, "Boy, stop what you doing. You ain't scaring nobody. You got bitch in you."

LIVED was hot after he read that last message. He was so mad he couldn't reply, and when he didn't, Lexi told Ciera, "Your turn."

"I see you like tough typing and hiding in bushes, just like a hoe."

LIVED didn't reply. He was furious.

Ciera sent another, "Don't get quiet now, BITCH, with your soft ass."

LIVED replied, "You don't want to see me. I will bring hell on earth."

Ciera sent, "LMFAO, that old ass line, hell on earth. Bitch, I'ma stomp your old ass and flip your wheelchair over, papa."

Yep, that last message did it. LIVED was heated. He made plans to visit Lexi and Ciera. He told his followers, "Send them little hoes a message, but no harm should come to them."

Omen said, "Now or later?"

LIVED said, "Now."

Five minutes later, Ciera and Lexi's car alarms went off, and the girls ran to the front door and saw broken windshields, busted windows, and "LIVED" written on the hood.

Chapter 59:

The

Confrontation

Ciera and Lexi looked at each other, then Brandy pointed down the street at a crowd of 20 people with hoods on, standing on the corner looking at them. Ciera and Lexi's phones both received messages from LIVED saying, "Them demons outside."

Lexi ran to the middle of the street and yelled, "What y'all want to do?"

Ciera ran out there with her and said, "Run up, bitches."

The 20 hooded people started walking towards them, and Brandy screamed, "MA!! We bout to fight," and ran to the street with Diana.

Brasia came to the door and saw the 20 people in hoods and told the girls, "Get y'all ass in here now, right now!"

Brandy said, "Ma, we got this," but Brasia and Janae ran and pulled the girls into the house and told them, "Look behind you." It was another 20 people in hoods coming from the back.

They all ran into the house and closed the door. When they looked out the window, all 40 of the hooded people were gone. LIVED sent a message to Lexi saying, "Don't run now." Then sent Ciera a message saying, "You left your shoe with your scary ass."

Chapter 60:

Unexpected Help

Brasia's phone rang; it was her husband Anthony calling back after she hung up to run outside. Anthony said, "What's going on at the house? I'm on my way home."

Brasia said, "Hurry up!"

After she hung up and the girls stopped breathing hard, they all looked at the principal and got quiet. Janae was standing with her back towards the window, and on the other side of the glass were two tall men in black hoodies staring at all of them.

Janae asked the girls, "Is there something behind me?"

Brasia said, "Yes, girl. Walk towards us slow, then turn around."

When the principal turned around, one of the hooded men showed them the chief police badge and walked away from the window, leaving the badge on the flower pot outside the window.

Brandy inboxed LIVED and asked, "Why are you messing with us? I thought you were my friend and had my back."

LIVED responded, "I'm sorry, friend. You right. I just get angry sometimes. I can't control my temper. I'm a fire starter. I'll stop."

Brandy sent a reply saying, "Thank you. Calm down, friend."

Chapter 61:

A Show of Force

They were terrified and shaking. Anthony pulled up and ran into the house, saying, "What the fuck going on in my house? What happened to the cars outside?" But right after he said that, a man knocked at the door.

Anthony opened the door and said, "Who the fuck are you?"

The man said, "I'm here to pick up those two cars for repairs and drop off these rentals until we are done. Free of charge, just sign here."

It was a Bentley coupe and a Bentley truck, so the girls ran and signed for them and grabbed the keys. LIVED sent Ciera and Lexi a message saying, "I'm sorry, and everything's paid for."

Anthony looked at Brasia and said, "Bae, what just happened?"

Janae shook her head, saying, "He is starting."

Ciera ran to the Bentley coupe and opened the door, seeing a Fendi bag with Brandy's name on it. Lexi ran to the Bentley truck and opened the door, noticing a Gucci bag with Brandy's name on it. Both girls yelled Brandy's name and held the bags in the air.

"Brandy! Brandy! Brandy! Look at these gifts with your name on them."

Brandy's alert went off with a message from LIVED saying, "The bags are your birthday gifts, friend."

Anthony asked, "Who sent these expensive gifts and what's starting, Janae? Brasia, what's going on?"

That's when Brandy said, "Ma, it's LIVED."

Conclusion

As the dust settles from the night's chaotic events, Brandy and her friends find themselves standing at the crossroads of a new beginning. The encounters with LIVED and his followers have not only tested their strength and resilience but also deepened their bonds and understanding of the real dangers that lurk behind the virtual façade of social media.

Brandy, Ciera, Lexi, and Diana sit together in the aftermath, their once naive outlooks transformed by the harsh realities they have faced. They have learned that true friendship is their strongest weapon, and their unity is their shield against any threat. Their journey has been filled with moments of fear, anger, and despair, but it has also been marked by courage, determination, and unwavering loyalty.

Principal Janae and Brasia, standing as pillars of support, reflect on their own past entanglements with LIVED. Their wisdom and experience have been crucial in guiding the girls through these turbulent times. As they prepare to move forward, they understand that the battle is far from over. LIVED is still out there, and his influence remains a looming threat.

Anthony, ever the protector, vows to keep his family safe. He knows that the real fight has only just begun, and he is ready to stand by his daughter and her friends as they face the challenges ahead.

As the sun rises, bringing with it a new day, the group stands united, stronger and more determined than ever. They have faced a formidable adversary and come out on the other side, but the journey is far from over. Their story continues, and with each step, they grow more prepared to confront whatever comes next.

To be continued...

The saga of Brandy, her friends, and their fight against the dark side of social media is only just beginning. The challenges they face will continue to test their limits, but with unity, courage, and determination, they are ready to take on whatever the future holds. Stay tuned for the next chapter in their journey, where new allies, deeper mysteries, and greater adversaries await.

Thank you for joining us on this journey through the digital maze. The story of **"Lived on Social Media"** continues, and we hope you will be there to witness the unfolding drama, the growing friendships, and the ultimate battle against those who seek to manipulate and control.

End of Book One

Stay tuned for Book Two in the **"Lived on Social Media"** series, where the adventure continues and the stakes are higher than ever.

Follow me @

FB

Acknowledgments

I extend my deepest gratitude to all those who have supported me on this creative journey. To my family and friends, thank you for your unwavering encouragement and belief in my vision. To my fans, your continued support and passion for my work have been a constant source of inspiration.

A special thanks to my editor and publishing team for their dedication, expertise, and meticulous attention to detail. Your hard work has been instrumental in bringing this project to life.

Lastly, to the readers—this book is for you. I hope these words ignite your imagination, provoke thought, and offer new perspectives. Your journey through these pages is the greatest honor an author can receive.

Author's Note

As an artist and storyteller, my aim is to explore the depths of the human experience through words and visuals. This book is an extension of that journey, blending narrative and design to create a unique and immersive experience. I invite you to step into this world with an open mind and heart, ready to see through a different lens.

Thank you for embarking on this journey with me.

Sincerely,

Caro Cartier

Made in the USA
Columbia, SC
02 May 2025

57472745R00136